Table of Contents

Introduction 3

Guidelines To Creating Balanced Homemade Dog Food 5

Dietary Supplements For Home-Fed Dogs 10

How to Ensure Proper Nutrition in Homemade Dog Food.... 14

How To Cook For Your Dog's 15

Common Mistakes When Cooking For Your Dog 16

An Alternative To Home Cooking 19

Tips To Improve Your Dog's Diet Today 20

Make Homemade Dog Food 31

Things You Need To Know Before Making Your Own
Homemade Dog Food 34

Recipe 36

Homemade Chicken & Vegetable Dog Food 36

Seeded Dog Biscuits 41

Lamb, Millet And Squash Stew 42

Beef, Barley And Broccoli Casserole 46

Doggy Breath Bones 47

Diy Homemade Dog Food 48

Healthy Homemade Dog Food 50

Diy: Healthy Homemade Dog Food 51

Easy Crockpot Dog Food 52

Crockpot with Ground Chicken 53

A Meal For You And Your Dog 53

Damn Delicious 55

Scooby's Stew 56

Beef & Veggie Crockpot Creation 57

Turkey & Veggie Mash 59

Meatballs 60

Raw Food Cakes 61

Chili 64

Meat Cakes 65

Meatloaf 67

Dinner Layer Cake 68

Crunchy Kibble 70

Spinach And Salmon Scramble 71

Vegan Happy Dog Bowl 72

Chicken Rice Balls 73

Food Pucks 75

Mini Omelettes 77

Chicken Rice Balls 78

Woof Loaf 80

Mini Omelettes 81

Homemade Chicken Dinner for Dogs 82

Homemade Fish Dinner for Dogs 83

Homemade Beef Dinner for Dogs 85

Homemade Doggy Dessert Dinner 86

Introduction

In the past few issues of Whole Dog book, I have offered critiques on homemade dog food diets in order to address the dog's health concerns or simply to optimize the dog's diet plan. To do this, I analyzed the cooked and raw homemade dog food diets and compared them to the National Research Council's guidelines for canine nutrition. I want to be clear, though: I don't believe this is a requirement for feeding home-cooked dog food. Just as with the diet you feed yourself and your family, feeding a wide variety of healthy foods in appropriate proportions should meet the needs of most healthy dogs. The best diet for dogs, in effect, is a diverse diet. Problems arise with how healthy dog food is interpreted. Too often, people think that they're feeding healthy homemade dog food, when key ingredients may be missing or are fed in excess. Here's how to make dog food at home, and specific guidelines to help ensure that the dog food diet you feed meets your individual dog's requirements. You do not want just one dog food recipe to follow you need several, and need to be comfortable mixing and matching ingredients,

It's important homemade dog food is "complete and balanced," meaning it meets all of the dog's nutritional needs. It is not important, however, that every meal be complete and balanced, unless you feed the same meal every day with little or no variation. Home-prepared dog diets that include a wide variety of foods fed at different meals rely on balance over time, not at every meal. Similar to the way humans eat, as long as your dog gets everything he needs spread out over each week or two, his diet will be complete and balanced. A human nutritionist would never expect someone to follow a single recipe with no variation, as veterinary nutritionist routinely do. Instead, a human would be given guidelines in terms of food groups and portion sizes. As long as your dog doesn't have a health problem that requires a very specific diet, homemade dog food should be the same way. Keep in mind that puppies are more susceptible to problems caused by nutritional deficiencies or excesses than adult dogs are.Large-breed puppies are particularly at risk from too much calcium prior to puberty.

Following are guidelines for feeding a raw or cooked home-prepared diet to healthy dogs. No single type of food, such as chicken, should ever make up more than half the diet. Except where specified, homemade food for dogs can be fed either raw or cooked. Leftovers from your table can be included as long as they're foods you would eat yourself, not fatty scraps.

Meat and Other Animal Products

Should always make up at least half of the diet. A raw diet for dogs can be excessively high in fat, which can lead to obesity. Another potential hazard of diets containing too much fat: If an owner restricts the amount fed (in order to control the dog's weight) too much, the dog may suffer deficiencies of other required nutrients. Unless your dog gets regular, intense exercise, use lean meats (no more than 10 percent fat), remove skin from poultry, and cut off separable fat. It's better to feed dark meat poultry than breast, however, unless your dog requires a very low-fat diet.

Raw Meaty Bones (optional)

If you choose to feed them, RMBs should make up one third to one half of the total diet. Use the lower end of the range if you feed bony parts such as chicken necks and backs, but you can feed more if you're using primarily meatier parts such as chicken thighs. Never feed cooked bones. Read a full report on raw meaty bones here.

Boneless Meat

Include both poultry and red meat. Heart is a good choice, as it is lean and often less expensive than other muscle meats.

Fish

Provides vitamin D, which otherwise should be supplemented. Canned fish with bones, such as sardines (packed in water, not oil), jack mackerel, and pink salmon, are good choices. Remove bones from fish you cook yourself, and never feed raw Pacific salmon, trout, or related species. You can feed small amounts of fish daily, or larger amounts once or twice a week. The total amount should be about one ounce of fish per pound of other meats (including RMBs).

Organs

Liver should make up roughly 5 percent of this category, or about one ounce of liver per pound of other animal products. Beef liver is especially nutritious, but include chicken or other types of liver at least occasionally as well. Feeding small amounts of liver daily or every other day is preferable to feeding larger amounts less often.

Eggs

Highly nutritious addition to any diet. Dogs weighing about 20 pounds can have a whole egg every day, but give less to smaller dogs.

Dairy

Plain yogurt and kefir are well tolerated by most dogs (try goat's milk products if you see problems). Cottage and ricotta cheese are also good options. Limit other forms of cheese, as most are high in fat.

Fruits and Vegetables

While not a significant part of the evolutionary diet of the dog and wolf, fruits and vegetables provide fiber that supports digestive health, as well as antioxidants and other beneficial nutrients that contribute to health and longevity.

Deeply colored vegetables and fruits are the most nutritious.

Starchy Vegetables

Veggies such as potatoes, sweet potatoes, and winter squashes (including pumpkin), as well as legumes (beans), provide carbohydrate calories that can be helpful in reducing food costs and keeping weight on skinny and very active dogs. Quantities should be limited for overweight dogs. Starchy foods must be cooked in order to be digestible.

Leafy Green and Other Non-Starchy Vegetables

These are low in calories and can be fed in any quantity desired. Too much can cause gas, and raw, cruciferous veggies such as broccoli and cauliflower can suppress thyroid function (cook them if you feed large amounts). Raw vegetables must be pureed in a food processor, blender, or juicer in order to be digested properly by dogs, though whole raw veggies are not harmful and can be used as treats. And while you're preparing these nutritious foods for your dog, consider boosting your own health by adding more veggies to your diet too!

Fruits

Bananas, apples, berries, melon, and papaya are good choices. Avoid grapes and raisins, which can cause kidney failure in dogs.

Grains

Controversial, as they may contribute to inflammation caused by allergies, arthritis, or inflammatory bowel disease (IBD); as well as seizures and other problems (it's not clear whether starchy vegetables do the same). Some grains contain gluten that may cause digestive problems for certain dogs. Many dogs do fine with grains, however, and they can be used to reduce the overall cost of feeding a homemade diet. Grains and starchy veggies should make up no more than half the diet. Good choices include oatmeal, brown rice, quinoa, barley, and pasta. White rice can be used to settle an upset stomach, particularly if overcooked with extra water, but it's low in nutrition and should not make up a large part of the diet. All grains must be well cooked.

Some supplements are required in addition to natural food for dogs. Others may be needed if you are not able to feed a variety of foods, or if you leave out one or more of the food groups above. In addition, the longer food is cooked or frozen, the more nutrients are lost. Here are some dog supplements to consider:

Calcium

Unless you feed RMBs, all homemade diets must be supplemented with calcium. The amount found in multivitamin and mineral supplements is not enough. Give 800 to 1,000 mg calcium per pound of food (excluding non-starchy vegetables). You can use any form of plain calcium, including eggshells ground to powder in a clean coffee grinder (1/2 teaspoon eggshell powder provides about 1,000 mg calcium). Animal Essentials' Seaweed Calcium provides additional minerals, as well. And here is a good list of calcium-rich foods your dog may like. Just please note this list is for humans and includes orange juice, which is not a good thing to give your dog as the acidity can cause stomach upset.

Oils

Most homemade diets require added oils for fat, calories, and to supply particular nutrients. It's important to use the right types of oils, as each supplies different nutrients.

Fish Oil

Fish oil for dogs provides EPA and DHA, omega-3 fatty acids that help to regulate the immune system and reduce inflammation. Give an amount that provides about 300 mg EPA and DHA combined per 20 to 30 pounds of body weight on days you don't feed fish. Note that liquid fish oil supplements often tell you to give much more than this, which can result in too many calories from fat.

Cod Liver Oil

Provides vitamins A and D as well as EPA and DHA. If you don't feed much fish, give cod liver oil in an amount that provides about 400 IUs vitamin D daily for a 100-pound dog (proportionately less for smaller dogs). Can be combined with other fish oil to increase the amount of EPA and DHA if desired.

Plant Oils

If you don't feed much poultry fat, found in dark meat and skin, linoleic acid, an essential omega-6 fatty acid, may be insufficient. You can use walnut, hempseed, corn, vegetable (soybean), or high-linoleic safflower oil to supply linoleic acid if needed. Add about one teaspoon of oil per pound of meat and other animal products, or twice that amount if using canola or sunflower oil. Olive oil and high-oleic safflower oil are low in omega-6 and cannot be used as a substitute, although small amounts can be added to supply fat if needed. Coconut oil provides mostly saturated fats, and can be used in addition to but not as a replacement for other oils.

Other Vitamins and Minerals

In addition to vitamin D discussed above, certain vitamins and minerals may be short in some homemade diets, particularly those that don't include organ meats or vegetables. The more limited the diet that you feed, the more important supplements become, but even highly varied diets are likely to be light in a few areas.

Vitamin E

All homemade diets I've analyzed have been short on vitamin E, and the need for vitamin E increases when you supplement with oils. Too much vitamin E, however, may be counterproductive. Give 1 to 2 IUs per pound of body weight daily.

Iodine

Too much or too little iodine can suppress thyroid function, and it's hard to know how much is in the diet. A 50-pound dog needs about 300 mcg (micrograms) of iodine daily. Kelp is high in iodine, though the amount varies considerably among supplements.

Multivitamin And Mineral Supplements

A multivitamin and mineral supplement will help to meet most requirements, including iodine and vitamins D and E, but it's important not to oversupplement minerals. If using the one-a-day type of human supplements, such as Centrum for Adults under 50, give one per 40 to 50 pounds of body weight daily. Note that most supplements made for dogs provide a reasonable amount of vitamins but are low in minerals, and so won't make up for deficiencies in the diet. Be cautious with small dogs; I've seen some supplements that recommend the same dosage for 10-pound dogs as for those weighing 50 or even 100 pounds. In those cases, the dosage is usually too high for the small dogs and should be reduced. Products made for humans are also inappropriate for small dogs.

Green Blends

Often containing alfalfa and various herbs, green blends may be especially helpful if you don't include many green vegetables in your dog's diet. You can also use a pre-mix that includes alfalfa and vegetables, such as The Honest Kitchen's Preference. Note most pre-mixes also supply calcium, so you should reduce or eliminate calcium supplements, depending on how much of the pre-mix you use.

How to Ensure Proper Nutrition in Homemade Dog Food

You'll want to keep an eye on health, make adjustments when needed, and don't overfeed them. You can also check with your veterinarian to make sure you are getting them what they need or if you need to add a supplement. There are three basic ingredients that you need to have for your dog to have a well rounded diet: some form of meat, a vegetable or two, and something for bulk such as rice or lentils. There are also some ingredients that you should never use when make dog food at home. Stay away from bacon and ham, onion, sugar, tomatoes, grapes, chocolate or most dairy products. Since the only dairy product dogs should consume is plain yogurt, you'll need to give your dog a calcium supplement as it is an important part of their diet. You can also find other additives to toss in to ensure your dog gets all the nutrients they need, like Nupro Dog Supplement or Pet Naturals of Vermont Daily Multi for Dogs. These supplements will ensure your dog's homemade diet is well balanced and good for them.

How To Cook For Your Dog's

Is cooking dog food at home really better for your pup? While there may be claims made to that effect, there's no hard scientific evidence to support it. "Owners are told by many sources that homemade food is superior to commercial products. However, there is no proof to support this claim," says Dr. Larsen. Larsen cautions dog owners to be aware of fearmongering within the pet food industry. This is often driven by myths about ingredient quality. While there are no scientifically-supported benefits to homemade diets, whole ingredient-based diets are better in the long term. Commercial foods are made to be complete and balanced, adds Dr. Bartges, albeit not the most exciting of meals. "Think of it as eating the same highly processed food for every meal, day after day, for years, " he affirms. Put that way, feeding your dogs a variety of whole foods makes a lot of sense. In fact, there are a multitude of reasons why you might want to prepare homemade foods for your dog, according to Dr. Larsen and Dr. Bartges. These include gaining control over your dog's diet, appeasing picky eaters, combatting food intolerance issues, concern over food recalls, or simply for the bond-building joy of preparing a home-cooked meal for your dog.

Common Mistakes When Cooking For Your Dog
Not Using Trusted Sources

"There are many inadequate, and sometimes dangerous recipes, available to owners," says Dr. Larsen. "There are now many studies demonstrating that most of these are not balanced." Some of these may cause deficiencies in your dog's diet, while others may lead to an excess of certain nutrients. To avoid encountering unhealthy or dangerous options Dr. Larsen and Dr. Bartges recommend avoiding generic recipes from books or online sources. Some so-called "nutrition experts" are without proper training, and may do more harm than good. Larsen and Bartges also suggest consulting BalanceIT.com, a site run by a board-certified veterinary nutritionist, to help create a semi-individualized diet.

Not Preparing Balanced Meals

When you don't prepare balanced meals that are individualized to your pet's needs, it can come at a cost. Nutrition deficiency (or excess) can lead to diseases, such as malnutrition or obesity, and can ultimately be fatal. "Each of the essential nutrients required by dogs has a specific role in the body. When they are provided in inadequate concentrations, the function is not optimal and suffering may result," explains Dr. Larsen. "Similarly, nutrient excesses can also cause illness. While the impact of an unbalanced diet may be mild and not even noticed or attributed to the diet by the owner, these problems can also be very severe, and pets do not always survive."

Relying On Multiple Diets To Create "Balance"

"Our study and my clinical experience has demonstrated that this approach is very unlikely to address problems since so many recipes share the same deficiencies," cautions Dr. Larsen.

Using Unsafe/Unhealthy Ingredients

There is a wide variety of unhealthy and unsafe foods to avoid when preparing meals for your dog. Potentially toxic ingredients are of special concern, including chocolate, xylitol, avocado, grapes, raisins, onions, garlic, and macadamia nuts. The above list is not exhaustive and other potential issues can arise if you're not careful about ingredients. So make sure to always be aware of which foods are safe for dogs. Additionally, cites Dr. Bartes, a certain type of heart disease called dilated cardiomyopathy has recently been reported in dogs eating homemade diets that are grain-free, legume-based, and high-fiber.

Not Following Recipes

"Most general recipes provide vague instructions for ingredients or preparation. This leaves the owner to interpret what type of meat to use, or which supplement product to buy," warns Dr. Larson, of the potential difficulty in following dog food recipes. Rather than improvising, it's important to run any questions by a veterinary nutritionist. That way, you'll be able to understand the impact alternative ingredients might have on your dog.

Understating the Impact of Dietary Changes

Ideally, when you go about creating a custom recipe for your dog, it will be under the guidance of a board-certified veterinary nutritionist. Factors like your dog's eating history, weight, and overall health should be considered. To make sure the food you're introducing is having the desired impact, you'll want to monitor your pet's health for changes over time.

An Alternative To Home Cooking

"Cooking for your pet is a process that's demanding on your time, labor, space, and finances," says Dr. Larsen. Home cooking is not for everyone, though, and it doesn't have to be. Another option to provide your dog with whole ingredients is to get carefully prepared ready-made meals. "There are commercial foods that can be purchased that contain whole ingredients that are pre-cooked. Which is very close to cooking," notes Dr. Bartges. So, while you might think that cooking for your dog is better for their health, it can be just as beneficial to purchase pre-prepared food that's made with the same principles in mind. Whichever method you choose, just to make sure you are always catering to your dog's individual health and nutrition needs.

Homemade Dog Food:

• Feed your dog a wide variety of foods from different food groups.

• Make sure you supplement your dog's homemade diet with calcium unless you feed raw meaty bones.

• Stick to lean meats and remove skin from the poultry you feed unless your dog is highly active.

• Keep in mind that the less variety of foods you feed, the more important supplements become.

• Review your homemade dog food diet plan with a veterinarian for approval.

Tips To Improve Your Dog's Diet Today
Discard The Marketing Hype And Take The Label Test

No matter how entertaining, relying on advertisements for nutritional information is not ideal. Why? Because the people that produce the ads didn't formulate the food. Their job is to make even the worst products appear healthy. Carefully examining the labels on your dog's food and treats will help you make more informed purchases. Product labels always list the ingredients in order, from the largest to the smallest. They may suit a diagnosed condition but can cause many other problems (and that's not even taking into account the cooking processes or packaging). Discuss the ingredients with the person or company recommending the products. If they can't explain what each ingredient is, its source, why and how it's good for dogs, then rely on your own research and judgment.

Avoid Feeding Shelf-Stable Foods As A Staple Diet

Thanks to clever marketing, the average consumer often overlooks the alarming reasons why processed food has a 12 to 24 month shelf life. Marketing has conditioned us to believe that shelf-stable foods provide everything dogs need to live long and healthy lives. Actually, the opposite is true. While there will always be the rare exception to the rule, don't count on your dog being one of them. Shelf-stable products have no live enzymes due to their industrial cooking processes. They're dead foods that rely on synthetic supplementation to meet the supposedly "balanced" nutritional standards set out by AAFCO. My gripe with these products is not that they exist, but the way they're marketed, as a staple, daily diet. After all, if we could pack all the nutrition the body needs for optimum health into a pellet or a can, then there would be thousands of companies out there producing human "food" and promoting it as a staple diet. Biscuits, kibble and canned foods have their place in shelters, charities, on long trips, or on occasions when we're pressed for time but they should not be fed as a staple diet.

Introduce Fresh Whole Foods

Fresh whole foods such as vegetables and fruit are full of live enzymes and will add a new dimension to your dog's health. Whole foods are also full of fiber, which aids digestion, encourages pooping and improves stools. Many of the nutrients are destroyed by the cooking processes that create shelf-stable foods. So the manufacturers add synthetic nutrients back into the products. These nutrients are synthetic imitations of those found in nature … and this is the vast difference between whole foods and industrially-produced foods. Unlike most synthetic nutrients, whole foods contain nutritional co-factors that work synergistically to help the body absorb, assimilate and make use of nutrients. You are not simply what you eat, but more importantly, you are what you can absorb.

Do Your Own Research On Safe Whole Foods For Dogs.

There are certain fruits and vegetables that dogs must avoid; also, you'll be amazed at which parts of the vegetables are the most nutritious. For example, broccoli stems contain more nutrients than the head, and beetroot leaves are full of goodness. Puree vegetables for maximum nutrient absorption or feed whole as a bone substitute for teeth and gum maintenance.

Feed A Variety Of Ingredients Rich In Antioxidants And Anti-Inflammatory Properties

Inflammation is a major cause of disease so it's important to research all ingredients in your dog's diet, along with the manufacturing processes. Inflammation is the leading cause of premature aging, not only in dogs, but in people, too. As you're probably now aware, processed commercial foods are inherently inflammatory. Pancreatitis and arthritis are common when you feed processed food too often. If you must use commercial food it's best to at least offset its ill effects by adding naturally anti-inflammatory whole foods into the mix. Whole foods high in antioxidants also help reduce inflammation in the body. Keep your dog young and healthy by feeding a variety of whole foods that are high in antioxidants and anti-inflammatories.

Avoid Cooking Meats

All species on the planet eat raw food except for humans. When we cook our food to please our palates, we lose many beneficial nutrients. It's the same when we cook food for our dogs. While certain whole foods may release more nutrients once cooked, it's best to avoid cooking meat for your dog whenever possible. Irrespective of the stated nutritional values, here's one of many reasons why commercial pet foods are fundamentally flawed

Use Certified Organic Vegetables And Fruit When Possible

Many of the non-organic fruit and vegetables on the market are genetically modified, and with no labeling laws in place it's impossible to know exactly what we and our dogs are eating. Although approved for human consumption, evidence suggests that genetically modified foods are not safe.

Wash Non-Organic Produce In Apple Cider Vinegar

We can't always afford or find organic produce so we have to make what we can get safer. Plants produce allelochemicals, which help prevent toxic substances including pesticides from penetrating their surface. You can scrub the pesticides off non-organic fruit and vegetables with a clean soft brush while soaking them in one part apple cider vinegar and four parts water for a minute, then rinsing.

Avoid Gluten

Have you ever joked about how smelly your dog's farts and poops are, Many dry pet foods contain gluten meal. This dried residue made from corn is added to pet food to prevent inferior, unstable fats from becoming rancid; this causes waste products to be retained and can strain the liver and kidneys. Corn gluten even in small quantities may harm your dog's organs; to make matters worse, GMO corn is often used in pet food

Replace Rice With Organic Green Lentils

Dogs don't need grains at all to be healthy. They don't eat them in the wild, and most are allergic to wheat. When a dog has an upset tummy it baffles me why many vets still recommend boiled chicken and rice. Even those commercial grain free dog foods typically contain grains. A great protein-rich substitute is green lentils. Just like rice, green lentils require boiling, so your preparation time is similar. It's best to soak them first and rinse before cooking, then rinse again after cooking. Lentils are one of the most nutritionally valuable leguminous plants. Lentils:

• Have the highest protein content.

• Are rich in fiber and minerals, particularly iron and magnesium.

• Rich in lysine, an essential amino acid that can help boost the immune system. It can prevent and treat cold sores, herpes and shingles in humans. Athletes also take it to improve performance.

Add Raw Coconut Oil As A Source Of Fat

Unlike animal fats and other vegetable fats, raw coconut oil (virgin cold-pressed) is truly unique. While it's high in saturated fat, it's a healthy saturated fat that mainly contains medium-chain fatty acids that the body doesn't store. Coconut oil can help you manage your dog's weight. Raw coconut oil goes straight to the liver where it gets converted into energy. The more energy your dog has, the more he exercises; the more he exercises, the leaner he stays; the leaner he stays, the less chance of obesity-related diseases.

Do Not Over-Feed And Limit Treats

Feed your dog according to whether he needs to gain or lose weight. If he's overweight, feed him earlier in the day so he has more time to work it off. If your dog needs to gain weight then feed more regularly and especially before bedtime, preventing the dog from burning off those calories. Within reason, don't worry about your dog being too skinny. It's ok for your dog to be very slim, especially in his younger, more active years. As he grows older, he'll gain weight more easily, so don't set him up for failure by trying to make him heavier too early – it will come naturally over time.   Just like marketing gurus once convinced mothers they should be putting snacks in their children's lunchboxes, they've tricked dog owners into believing that giving our dogs treats is normal.

Get Creative For Teeth And Gum Health

Some commercial treats claim to benefit teeth and gum health but their unhealthy ingredients and cooking processes can cause other health problems. Marketing does it again. If you ask any dentist how to best keep teeth plaque-free and gums healthy they'll recommend brushing. The same rules apply for dogs. It isn't always possible or practical to brush your dog's teeth so bones come in a close second. Gnawing on raw bones will help keep your dog's teeth sparkling white. Another good solution is to give your dog whole foods like carrots and zucchini to chomp on. You see, it's all about the rubbing and sloughing action on the teeth. You can make fresh treats for your dog to gnaw on to help remove plaque. Try cutting some holes in vegetables and cover them with melted raw coconut oil. Place in the freezer for five minutes then serve. These treats can also satisfy a dog's need to grind and chomp, and they aren't as harsh on teeth as bones. Be warned – there will be bits of vegetables everywhere. But that's ok, you're not feeding these primarily for nutrition purposes. In the unlikely event your dog rejects these natural treats at first, don't give up. Play games with the treats, throwing them to encourage a fetching game, or even play hide and seek. Raw coconut oil also acts as a wonderful canine toothpaste because it has antiviral, antibacterial, and antifungal properties – plus most dogs love the taste. Allowing your dog to lick hardened coconut oil off a bowl for 20 seconds after each meal is a great way to help with bad breath.

Rethink Your Water

Water is the most important aspect of a healthy diet yet it's the most overlooked. There are well over 150 chemicals in most tap waters, depending on where you live. We can argue all day about the safety of that healthy, naturally-occurring stuff called fluoride, or we can shift our focus towards its nasty, toxic waste version that's in our water supply. Hydrofluorosilicic acid. 97% of Europe refuses to put it in their water supply. It's a byproduct of fertilizer manufacturing and it contains traces of arsenic and lead, and also increases the body's uptake of aluminium. Of course all homes should have a water filter to remove unwanted chemicals but in an ideal scenario having pure water to begin with is better. I prefer to pour an imported alkaline water for my dogs (Saka is a good brand if you can find it) and it's the only water they drink. While feeding alkaline water to dogs may go against the grain, I can see the benefits. A very cost effective alternative to water filters is Willard Water one of the most unusual products you'll ever find. In essence it is just water, but add a few drops of it into your dog's water bowl and special things start to happen. It purifies water, makes it alkaline, and also helps with nutrient absorption, among many other benefits.

Wash Bowls With Vinegar

A good white vinegar is a chemical-free alternative to commercial cleaning products. Among other things, you can use it to wash your dishes and clean surfaces, including dog bowls and floors. It disinfects and is odorless when dry. Dogs can be sensitive to commercial cleaning products so replace as many of these as possible with natural alternatives. Apart from vinegar, you can Google search organic and safe, ready-made cleaning products.

Take Charge

You know your dog better than anyone so it makes sense that you should be in control of your dog's diet. I couldn't even cook for myself when I started making food for Augustine but it didn't take long to get the hang of it – and now she's an icon of health.

Make Homemade Dog Food
Start With a Good Recipe

Many dog food recipes fall short in certain nutrients, especially iron, copper, calcium, and zinc. Even some recipes created by veterinarians don't measure up. The University of California, Davis, School of Veterinary Medicine tested 200 recipes, many written by vets. The researchers found most of the recipes were short on some essential nutrients. The best way to make sure a recipe has what it takes is to choose one created by an expert with training in dog nutrition, says Jennifer Larsen, DVM, PhD. That might be a certified pet nutritionist or a PhD-trained animal nutritionist with experience making pet food. Your vet should be able to point you in the right direction. Your pet needs protein (animal meat, seafood, dairy, or eggs), fat (from meat or oil) and carbohydrates (grains or vegetables).

He also needs calcium (from dairy or an ingredient such as egg shells), and essential fatty acids (from certain plant oils, egg yolks, oatmeal, and other foods). And if that's not enough to consider, if your dog has a health problem, he may need a special diet. You may need a pet nutrition expert to create custom recipes.

Prepare the Recipe Right

Tempted to experiment in the kitchen? Save it for yourself. It's best not to improvise when you cook for your pooch. Follow the recipe. Altering it can have unintended effects. For example, cooking chicken with or without skin and bone changes the recipe's nutrient profile, Larsen says. You might also add or subtract calories without meaning to. Don't swap ingredients. Some ingredients seem similar but don't provide the same nutrition. For example, corn, canola, and walnut oil provide certain essential fatty acids that olive oil and coconut oil don't. By making swaps, "you could very easily unbalance the diet," Larsen says. Buy a food scale. They are much more accurate than measuring cups, especially for measuring meat. Cook all animal products to kill bacteria that could make your pooch sick. Cook grains, beans, and starchy vegetables to make them easier to digest. Never add foods that are toxic to dogs. These include chocolate, grapes, raisins, onions, garlic, avocados, and Macadamia nuts. If you want to mix things up, do it with the treats you feed. Offer dog-safe fresh fruits and vegetables as treats.

Add the Right Supplements

Even the best recipes often don't provide enough of certain nutrients, such as calcium. Your pup needs supplements if you're feeding him from scratch. Which ones depend on which nutrients are missing from his meals. A good recipe should include specific supplement instructions. If you're unsure, talk to a pet nutritionist.

Make Sure the Diet's Working

After your dog's been dining on your kitchen creations for 2 to 3 weeks, take him to the vet to make sure he's not gaining or losing too much weight. If his weight is changing, check it again in a couple of weeks. Take your pooch for a checkup twice a year. The vet can look at his skin, coat, body condition, and "any type of problems that might be happening as the result of the diet," Larsen says.

There Are Lots Of Good Resources For Recipes

Want to get cooking but don't know where to begin? Cookbooks are usually a better bet than random recipes you can find online, says Julia Hansen, DVM, Program Chair of the Veterinary Technology Program at Argosy University. The recipes are more likely to have been formulated to meet a dog's nutritional needs. They'll also be more likely to be free of ingredients that dogs shouldn't eat including raisins, grapes, onions, garlic, and avocado. (And of course, chocolate.) One reputable dog cookbook, which includes veterinarian-reviewed recipes for cooked and raw meals as well as treats is Home Cooking for Your Dog, Or, try the online nutritional tool Balance it. It offers free, vet-created recipes for dogs (as well as cats). You can also enter your own recipe to see how it stacks up, nutritionally. (While you're at it, consider making one of these homemade dog treat recipes that are healthier, safer and cheaper than store-bought.)

But You Should Talk To Your Vet First

Packaged dog food is formulated to meet the essential nutritional guidelines that your pup needs to be healthy and maintain the right weight. So before you start whipping up homemade food, talk to your vet to make sure that what you're serving will meet your dog's needs. "You want to make sure that your food has the appropriate protein to carb balance. And that depends on the size and age of your pet," says Hansen. Getting the right mix of vitamins and minerals matters, too, especially for nutrients like calcium and phosphorus. Low calcium can make your dog's bones more fragile and put him at risk for fractures, Hansen says. And too much phosphorus can have a negative impact on kidney function.

Once You Go Homemade, You Won't Go Back

Make sure you're fully committed to cooking for your dog before you start feeding her homemade fare. Once she's had a taste of the fresh stuff, there's a good chance that she'll have zero interest in eating kibble, says Christine Filardi, holistic pet chef and author of Home Cooking for Your Dog, Even if you haven't had time to go shopping and cook a new batch of food. (Plus, switching back and forth could irritate your dog's stomach, Filardi says.) Make an effort to plan ahead, or put a system into place so you always have a batch of food on hand. For instance, try prepping your dog's food for the week on Sunday, just like you'd meal prep for yourself. And if you know that you have a crazy week coming up and won't have time to cook, make a double batch and stick it in the freezer. And if all else fails, Keep your kitchen stocked with a few non-perishable ingredients for fast, easy meals when you're in a pinch, Filardi recommends. Think canned fish (like mackerel or sardines), canned pumpkin, and frozen berries or greens. "This isn't rocket science, so don't put pressure on yourself," she says. "If you have to whip up a box of instant rice and throw in a can of fish once in a while, it's fine."

Recipe

Homemade Chicken & Vegetable Dog Food
Ingredients

- 6 lbs. chicken breast meat, skinless, boneless (raw)

- 4 lbs. chicken thigh meat, skinless, boneless (raw)

- 7 oz. chicken liver

• 3 oz. chicken gizzards

• 3 oz. chicken hearts

• 6 eggs (raw)

• 24 oz. chicken stock (made from cooking the chicken)

• 3.75 oz. canned sardines in spring water, drained

Vegetables and Fruit

• 1½ lbs. sweet potatoes (unpeeled)

• 10 oz. carrots (unpeeled)

• 8 oz. cabbage or broccoli, brussels sprouts, etc.

• 4 oz. kale or other leafy greens

• 8 oz. butternut squash or similar squash

• 4 oz. blueberries (or other kind of berry, fresh or frozen)

• 12 oz. green beans or peas

• 6 oz. pumpkin purée

• ¼ cup parsley, stems included

• 8 oz. apple

Seeds and Grain

• 6 oz. quick-cooking oats (dry)

• 8 oz. cooked garbanzo beans (aka chickpeas)

• 3 tbsp. ground pumpkin seeds

• 3 tbsp. ground sunflower seeds

• 1 tbsp. chia seeds

• 1 tbsp. ground flax seed

Supplements

• 1 Vitamin E, 100 IU

• 4½ tsp. (17 g) calcium carbonate made from eggshells

• 1¼ tsp. taurine powder (NOW)

• 1 tablet zinc copper (Solaray)

• 2 tablets ground Up & Up Woman's Daily Multivitamin (Target)

• ¼ tsp. kelp powder (NOW); comes with tiny spoon;

• 10 of its spoonfuls equal ¼ tsp.

Instructions

• Using an electric pressure cooker, cook 4 oz. dried garbanzo beans in 2 c. of water, using the "bean/chili" setting on high pressure for 20 minutes. This will produce 8 oz. of cooked beans. Or you can use drained canned garbanzo.

• Drain and cool the beans. Empty the pot.

• Cut the chicken into large chunks, trimming most of the fat. Roughly chop the organ meat (liver, etc.). Place half of the meats into the pot with 1 ½ cups of water and cook on low pressure for 10 mins. Let the pressure release naturally. Transfer the chicken to a large bowl or pan. Drain the broth.

• Return 1 ½ c. of broth to the cooker and add the rest of the raw meat. Repeat the cooking process.

• Reserve the broth.

• Finely dice/process the sweet potatoes and the other vegetables and fruit, including the parsley, using a food processor, or by hand. Grind the cooked (or canned) garbanzos in a food processor.

• Place half of the cooked chicken back into the pot, along with 12 oz. of the reserved chicken broth and half of the vegetables, and cook for 5 mins. on low pressure; use the manual release. (Since the chicken has been cooked, ingredients only need to be cooked lightly hence the shorter time.)

• Add 3 beaten eggs, 4 oz. of ground-up garbanzos, half of the ground seeds (excluding the flax seed, which is heat sensitive and will be added later), half the sardines, and 3 oz. uncooked oats.

• Stir together. The chicken and other ingredients must be mixed in well.

• Keep warm in the covered pot for a few minutes (time for the eggs and oats to cook). Then remove the inner pot from the cooker and let the food cool.

• Note: The oats, eggs and chia also act as binding/thickening agents.

• Move that batch into a large bowl, then repeat the cooking process for the second batch of ingredients.

• Stir in and dissolve the supplements and ground flax seed in a small amount of the stock; if using the vitamins in capsules, be sure to break or cut in half, and grind the tablets. Sprinkle half on each batch of cooled food and incorporate it well. It is very important that all the ingredients are thoroughly mixed.

• Use the pulse function on a food processor to blend everything together. This will ensure that all ingredients have been equally dispersed and the food has a mushy, thickly puréed consistency. Or do it manually using a food masher, or even by hand (akin to making meat loaf).

• Be sure to break apart the pieces of chicken (which should already be well-shredded) and mix with everything else extra-well.

Seeded Dog Biscuits
Ingredients

• 1 1/2 cups oat flour (grind the oats yourself for maximum freshness)

• 1/2 cup unsweetened applesauce (canned or homemade)

• 1/3 cup ground up hemp seeds (or a mix of a variety of ground seeds like flax, pumpkin, sunflower, etc.)

• 1/4 cup olive, canola (non GMO) or grapeseed oil (or any neutral vegetable oil).

Instructions

• Mix all of ingredients in a bowl. Knead the mixture a few times (you can do this in the bowl). Form dough into a ball and refrigerate for 30 minutes. Generously dust working space and rolling pin in oat flour. Roll out the dough, about 1/4-inch thick. Cut the dough into rectangles or cookie-cutter shapes. Place on a parchment lined-baking sheet, evenly spaced. Bake at 350 degrees for 30 minutes, or until hardened and cooked through

Lamb, Millet And Squash Stew

Ingredients

• ½ tsp olive oil

• 500g stewing lamb

• 1 garlic clove, finely chopped (optional)

• 500ml stock (unsalted) or water

• 80g millet

• 300g butternut squash, peeled, deseeded and cut into 1cm dice

• 100g peas, fresh or frozen

• 2 tbsp mint, finely chopped

Instructions

• Warm the oil in a heavy saucepan over a medium-high heat and add the lamb. Cook, stirring from time to time, for five minutes. Lower the heat, add the garlic, if using, and stir for a minute. Pour in the stock, bring to a simmer, cover and cook for 30 minutes.

• Add the millet and squash and cook for a further 30 minutes, stirring from time to time, until the meat is very tender. Add the peas, cook for five minutes more, remove from the heat and stir in the mint. Cool before serving.

• If you like, cook this in a slow cooker for around eight hours, or in a pressure cooker on high for 25-30 minutes.

• It will keep sealed in the refrigerator for three to four days, or in the freezer for four months.

Ingredients

For the lamb

- ½ tsp olive oil

- 2 carrots, scrubbed and cut into 5mm dice

- 1 celery stick, finely diced

- 1 garlic clove, finely chopped

- 500g minced lamb

- 200ml goat's milk

- 400g tinned chopped tomatoes

- 400ml chicken, lamb or beef stock (unsalted) or water

- 1 tsp rosemary, finely chopped

- 150g peas, fresh or frozen

For The Mash

- 1kg sweet potatoes, peeled and cut into 3cm chunks

- 1 tsp olive oil

Instructions

• For the lamb, warm the oil in a heavy saucepan or casserole over a medium heat. Add the carrots and celery and stir until softened, about five minutes. Add the garlic and stir for a minute.

• Turn up the heat a bit and tip in the lamb, breaking it up with a fork. Cook, stirring, until the meat is browned, about 10 minutes. Pour in the milk and simmer, stirring from time to time, until the milk has almost evaporated, then tip in the tomatoes, stock (or water), and rosemary.

• Simmer for one hour, stirring from time to time and topping up with water if it looks dry, until you have a rich, meaty sauce. Add the peas, cook for a minute or two, then remove from the heat.

• While the lamb is cooking, make the mash. Tip the sweet potatoes into a pan with enough water to cover. Bring to a simmer and cook until the sweet potatoes are tender, about 15-20 minutes. Drain and mash with the olive oil.

• Spoon some cooled lamb into your dog's bowl with some cooled sweet potato mash. Any leftovers will keep in the refrigerator for three to four days, or in the freezer for up to four months.

Ingredients

- ½ tsp olive oil

- 600g stewing beef

- 2 carrots, scrubbed and cut into 5mm dice

- 1 celery stick, cut into 5mm dice (if you have leaves, chop them finely and add them at the end)

- 400g tinned chopped tomatoes

- 400ml homemade stock (unsalted) or water

- 80g pearl barley, rinsed

- 175g broccoli, roughly chopped into small pieces

- 2 tbsp parsley or oregano, leaves and stems finely chopped

Instructions

- Warm the oil in a heavy saucepan over a medium heat and add the beef, carrots and celery and cook, stirring for five minutes.

• Tip in the tomatoes and stock or water and bring to a simmer. Add the barley, return to a simmer, lower the heat, cover, and cook for one hour, until the beef is tender and the barley is cooked.

• Add the broccoli and cook for a further 10 minutes. Remove from the heat, stir in the herbs and any celery tops you might have. Cool before serving.

• If you like, cook this in a slow cooker for around eight hours, or in a pressure cooker on high for 25-30 minutes.

• It will keep sealed in the refrigerator for three to four days, or in the freezer for four months.

Doggy Breath Bones
Ingredients

• Big bunch of parsley, about 70g, stalks and leaves finely chopped

• 1 large carrot, about 130g, grated

• 60g cheddar, grated

• 300g buckwheat flour or brown rice flour, plus a little more for dusting later on

• 70ml olive oil About

• 50ml hot water

Instructions

• Preheat the oven to 180C/Gas 4.

• Mix together the parsley, carrot, cheese and flour until well combined. Trickle over the olive oil and stir in the water. Turn the mixture out onto a lightly floured surface and knead until you have a firm dough. Roll out to 5mm thick and cut out with a bone-shaped cookie cutter.

• Lay the dough bones on baking trays and bake in the preheated oven for 22-24 minutes, until crisp and starting to brown slightly around the edges. Cool on a wire rack before serving.

• The bones will keep for a month in an airtight jar, or you can freeze them for up to four months.

Diy Homemade Dog Food

Ingredients

• 1 1/2 cups brown rice

• 1 tablespoon olive oil

• 3 pounds ground turkey

• 3 cups baby spinach, chopped

• 2 carrots, shredded

• 1 zucchini, shredded

• 1/2 cup peas, canned or frozen

Instructions

• In a large saucepan of 3 cups water, cook rice according to package instructions; set aside.

• Heat olive oil in a large stockpot or Dutch oven over medium heat. Add ground turkey and cook until browned, about 3-5 minutes, making sure to crumble the turkey as it cooks.

• Stir in spinach, carrots, zucchini, peas and brown rice until the spinach has wilted and the mixture is heated through, about 3-5 minutes.

• Let cool completely.

Ingredients:

• 3 lbs ground turkey (or any protein)

• 1 cup uncooked millet (or any other whole grain: quinoa, rice, pasta)

• 1 tbs olive oil

• 1 carrot, shredded

• 1 zucchini, shredded

• 1 squash, shredded

• 1 apple, chopped

• 1 tbs calcium powder

• 1/4 cup unsweetened coconut flakes or coconut oil

• 1/2 cup pumpkin puree (canned or homemade)

Instructions

• Bring 1 cup of whole grain to boil in a pot of water. I overcook it so that it's soft and easily digestible. Drain.

• While that's boiling, shred/chop the veggies.

Ingredients

- 3 lbs ground turkey (or any protein)

- 1 cup uncooked millet (or any other whole grain: quinoa, rice, pasta)

- 1 tbs olive oil

- 1 carrot, shredded

- 1 zucchini, shredded

- 1 squash, shredded

- 1 apple, chopped

- 1 tbs calcium powder

- 1/4 cup unsweetened coconut flakes or coconut oil

- 1/2 cup pumpkin puree (canned or homemade)

Instructions

- Bring 1 cup of whole grain to boil in a pot of water. I overcook it so that it's soft and easily digestible. Drain.

- While that's boiling, shred/chop the veggies.

• Cook ground turkey with olive oil and drain excess juices.

• Mix everything together! No need to cook the veggies. The cooked turkey and whole grain will warm them up a bit.

Ingredients

• 2 1/2 pounds ground beef

• 1 1/2 cups brown rice

• 1 (15-ounce) can kidney beans, drained and rinsed

• 1 1/2 cups chopped butternut squash

• 1 1/2 cups chopped carrots

• 1/2 cup peas, frozen or canned

Instructions:

• Stir in ground beef, brown rice, kidney beans, butternut squash, carrots, peas and 4 cups water into a 6-qt slow cooker.

• Cover and cook on low heat for 5-6 hours or high heat for 2-3 hours, stirring as needed.

• Let cool completely.

Crockpot with Ground Chicken

Ingredients

• 3 lbs lean ground chicken

• 1 cup butternut squash I use frozen, precut

• 15 oz can kidney beans drained

• 1 cup peas

• 1 cup green beans

• 1 cup carrots sliced or diced

• 1 1/2 cup uncooked rice

• 4 cups of water

Instructions

• Throw everything in crockpot.

• Cook on high for 4 hours or low for 6 hours, stirring occasionally.

A Meal For You And Your Dog

Ingredients:

• 2 tablespoons olive oil

• 2 salmon portions

• 1 squash

• 1 head of broccoli (with stem)

• 3 potatoes (any kind)

• 2 carrots

Instructions

• Cut broccoli stem, peel carrots and cut squash. Keep the peelings as this is for your dog. Mix together and steam in rice cooker or bake in oven. Check out Rocky's favorite rice cooker.

• Air fry potato shavings after pouring in 1 table spoon olive oil in air fryer (or place in oven.

• Pan fry salmon in 1 table spoon olive oil with skin on. Start with skin side down on the pan at a medium temp. After flipping, pull off crisp salmon skin off both pieces of salmon and place in dog bowl.

• Once everything is finished cooking mix all together in dog bowl. Chop to small bitesize for ease and a cleaner floor

Damn Delicious
Ingredients

• 1 1/2 cups brown rice

• 2 carrots, shredded

• 1 tablespoon olive oil

• 1 zucchini, shredded

• 3 pounds ground turkey

• 1/2 cup peas, canned or frozen

• 3 cups baby spinach, chopped

Instructions

• In a large saucepan of 3 cups water, cook rice according to package instructions; set aside.

• Heat olive oil in a large stockpot or Dutch oven over medium heat. Add ground turkey and cook until browned, about 3-5 minutes, making sure to crumble the turkey as it cooks.

• Stir in spinach, carrots, zucchini, peas and brown rice until the spinach has wilted and the mixture is heated through, about 3-5 minutes.Let cool completely.

Scooby's Stew
Ingredients

• 1 1/2 cups brown rice

• 2 carrots, shredded

• 1 tablespoon olive oil

• 1 zucchini, shredded

• 3 pounds ground turkey

• 1/2 cup peas, canned or frozen

• 3 cups baby spinach, chopped

Instructions

• Place ingredients in slow cooker in order listed, covering chicken completely with vegetables

• Cook 5 hours on high or 8 hours on low

• Remove from slow cooker, shred chicken and stir into rice and veggie mixture until evenly distributed.

• Store covered in fridge for up to three days or freeze in single-serve portions.

Beef & Veggie Crockpot Creation

Ingredients

• 2 1/2 pounds ground beef

• 1 1/2 cups chopped butternut squash

• 1 1/2 cups brown rice

• 1 1/2 cups chopped carrots

• 1 (15-ounce) can kidney beans, drained and rinsed

• 1/2 cup peas, frozen or canned

Instructions

• Stir in ground beef, brown rice, kidney beans, butternut squash, carrots, peas and 4 cups water into a 6-qt slow cooker.

• Cover and cook on low heat for 5-6 hours or high heat for 2-3 hours, stirring as needed.

• Let cool completely.

Chicken & Veggie Slow Cooker

Ingredients

• 2 1/2-3 lbs boneless skinless chicken thighs and breasts

• 2 c. frozen peas

• 1 sweet potato, cubed

• 1 large or

• 2 medium apples, cored and cubed (no seeds)

• 2 carrots, sliced

• 1 can of kidney beans, drained and rinsed

• 2 c. frozen green beans

• 2 tbsp olive oil

Instructions

• Place meat in the crockpot and add water so that it just covers the chicken. Then, add potato, carrots, kidney beans, green beans, and apple.

• Cook on low for 8-9 hours, when it is about finished, add the frozen peas and cook for another 30 minutes.

• When finished, drain off excess liquid, add olive oil, and stir to mash (or place in a food processor).

• When cooled, scoop daily servings into individual ziploc bags and freeze. Each night, remove one bag from the freezer and place in the fridge to defrost overnight.

Turkey & Veggie Mash

Ingredients

• 2 pounds lean ground turkey

• 1 cup cauliflower florets

• 2 tablespoons raw turkey or chicken liver, finely diced or pureed

• 1/2 zucchini, sliced

• 2 medium carrots, coarsely chopped

• 2 tablespoons olive oil

• 1 cup broccoli florets

Instructions

• Add 1 1/2 cups water to a double boiler, place carrots in a steam basket over the pot and cover. Heat until boiling, reduce heat to a low boil and steam until carrots start to get tender, about 10 minutes. In the meantime, add the turkey and liver to a large skillet and cook on medium-high heat until done and there's no more pink color. Drain off any fat and discard.

• Add broccoli, cauliflower, and zucchini, and continue steaming until all vegetables are tender, but not mushy, about 6-8 minutes. Allow vegetables to cool slightly then either chop in a food processor use a knife. The size of the vegetables will depend on the consistency preferred. We usually pulse about three times in the food processor and get the vegetables to a finely chopped consistency, similar to canned dog food.

• Add chopped vegetables to the turkey and liver, stir to combine. Add the olive oil and toss to combine with the turkey & veggie mixture. Allow to cool before dividing into freezer safe containers.

Meatballs
Ingredients:

- 10 lbs ground beef (lean)

- 3 slices of bread, cubed small

- 2 cups of oat bran

- 4 eggs

- 3 cans pumpkin pureeSome salt

- 4 carrots, boiled/steamed and mashedFlourLeaves of

- 4 kale stalk chopped finely

Instructions

- Put all ingredients in a large bowl. Mix them all together and form them into any size of balls you'd like.

- Dredge the balls lightly in the flour, shaking off any excess.

- Put them in 400 degree oven until done. Bake time will depend on the size of your balls; usually mine only take about 25 min. (Mine are about the size of a muscadine or those donut holes)

Raw Food Cakes

Ingredients

- 2 cups rice (brown or white)Other fruit: peaches, pears, plums are all okay for dogs and nutritious.

- 4 cups unsalted, no-onion chicken broth1 green beans (sometimes more.)

- 2 large yams, steamed or baked (I use the microwave to make it quickly)

- 1 snap peas, or whatever peas in the pod you have around

- 2 cups pumpkin puree (in season)1 snap peas, or whatever peas in the pod you have around1 large bunch parsley

- 12 eggshells or more (baked to dry, grind in small "coffee grinder")

- 8 large carrots

- 9 eggs, poached lightly then cooled

- 1/4 head cabbage (optional warning: ground up cabbage has a strong smell)

- 1 c. peanut butter (more or less I use this as a binder & for protein)

- 1 broccoli head

• 2/3 cup nutritional yeast (lots of vitamins)

• 1/3 cup dog multiple vitamin powder6 celery stalks

• 1 cup flax meal (if you just have the seed, finely grind it in food processor)

• 1 large zucchini and/or yellow summer squash (in season)

• 1 cup raw pumpkin seeds or raw almonds (finely processor)

• 4 large apples (more is good)

• 2 cups rolled oats, optional (1/2 ground in food processor, 1/2 whole)

• 1 cranberries (in season, sometimes more)

• 1/2 cup olive oil1 blueberries (in season. These turn food gray. If it bothers you, skip blueberries)

• 1/2 cup rose hips, dried and ground in coffee grinder

Instructions:

• Cook rice in broth til done (the way you usually cook rice — I use a rice cooker) Then, let cool

• Puree the yams in food processor, skin and all.

• Finely chop or grind the fruits and vegetables in a food processor (the finer the more digestible.) I do one thing at a time in my Cuisinart and save time by NOT washing it out between ingredients. It doesn't matter anyway since all of the ingredients get mixed together.

• Put all of the ingredients into a very large bowl (I use a huge bread bowl my brother gave me over 20 years ago) Add the rest of the ingredients and stir well. (I use my hands to mix it there is a lot here.)

• Mix with your hands or a spoon til all the ingredients have been incorporated into a squishy, moist glop.

• Put waxed paper or parchment paper on 2 large cookie sheets. Scoop out measured amounts of the mixture in "balls" or "cakes" and place on waxed paper close together. Freeze until hard. Put the cakes in airtight freezer bags and thaw as needed.

Chili

Ingredients:

• 4 Carrots

• 1 Can of tomato paste

• 2 Tbsp ButterBeef Broth (NO SALT)

• 1 lb Ground BeefOptional Can of Corn

Instructions:

• First you need to boil the macaroni. In a frying pan, cook the beef.

• Add butter, carrots, corn and tomato paste to your beef and cook for about 5 minutes.

• Then add your beef mixture to your casserole dish, add your beef broth.

• After that, put in oven at 350 degrees and cook for half an hour.

Meat Cakes

Ingredients:

• 1 1/2 cups brown riceMarket Pantry Ground Beef

• 1-lb Pkg3 cups water

• 8 eggs

• 2 large potatoes, grated

• 1 dash salt

• 4 large carrots, grated

• 1/4 cup olive oil

• 2 large celery stalks, chopped

• 1 1/2 cups regular rolled oats

Instructions

• Preheat oven to 400 degrees F (205 degrees C). Grease 36 cups of 3 large muffin tins.

• In a medium saucepan, combine the rice with water. Bring to a boil over high heat, uncovered, and cook 10 minutes. Reduce heat to low, cover, and simmer 20 minutes. Remove from heat, let cool several minutes, then fluff with a fork and set aside.

• In a large bowl, combine the potatoes, carrots, celery, ground beef, and eggs. Mix ingredients together using your hands or a sturdy spoon. Add salt, olive oil, rolled oats, and rice; mix well.

• Fill each muffin cup with some of the meat mixture, and pat down the to make it firm. Bake 45 minutes, or until surface feels set. Cool on a rack 10 minutes or longer.

• Remove the meat cakes by turning the muffin tin upside down over a sheet of aluminum foil. Tap each muffin cup to release the cake. Refrigerate or freeze in sealed plastic bags.

Meatloaf
Ingredients

• 1 lbs. lean ground beef

• 1 ½ cups grated mixed vegetables (use your dog's favorite veggies – Amy used broccoli, carrots and apple)

• 2 eggs½ cup cottage cheese

• 1 ½ cups rolled oats

Instructions

• Preheat oven to 350 degrees F.

• Hand-mix all ingredients in a bowl until combined thoroughly. Press evenly into a loaf pan.

• Bake for 40 minutes.

• Refrigerate or freeze in slices for easy serving.

Ingredients:

• 1 kg (2.2 lbs) Chicken

• 1 medium Apple

• 1/2 cup of carrots

• 1 Egg shell and all

• 1/2 cup of peas

• 1 cup of Brown rice

• 1/2 cup of sweet corn

Instructions

• Preheat oven to 170º C

• Pop the chopped carrots, peas, and sweetcorn in a pot to cook and soften.

• Peel and chop apple into small pieces

• Minced the chicken in a food processor (or just buy it already minced)

• Cook brown rice according to package

• Mush vegetable mix

• Pulverize a whole egg so that shell is totally crushed.

• Blend chopped apple, egg and chicken together in a mixing bowl

• Mix vegetable melee and rice together in bowl

Instructions

• Grease a cake pan or line with baking paper.

• Take 1/2 of chicken mixture and place in bottom of cake pan.

• Take about 2/3 of the veggie and rice mix and place on top of chicken base

• use the rest of chicken mixture and place on top of the veggie and rice mix

• Top up the cake with the last of the veggie mixture

• Pop it into your pre-heated oven and cook for 35 minutes or until juices run clear

• Let cool and then remove from pan and slice a piece of posh chicken heaven for your dog.

Crunchy Kibble

Ingredients

• 6 cups of flour white, whole wheat or oat

• 3 large eggs or four medium eggs

• 1 cup of powdered milk

• 1/3 cup baking oil

• 2 mixing bowls

• 2-1/2 cups of milk, broth or water

• 2 wooden spoons

Instructions:

• Preheat your oven to 350 degrees. Spray a cookie sheet with a light coating of baking spray and set it aside.

• Pour the flour and powdered milk into a mixing bowl. Stir with a wooden spoon to combine the ingredients and set the bowl aside.

• Mix the eggs, baking oil and liquid choice in the second mixing bowl with a wooden spoon until the ingredients are thoroughly combined.

• Combine the dry ingredients with the wet ingredients and mix into a thick, moist dough, similar to bread. Add any additional ingredients that you wish to mix in, such as the cheese, shredded meat, pureed fruits or vegetables. If the dough is too dry, add some additional liquid; if it is too wet, add some additional flour to get a smooth consistency.

• Use the wooden spoon to spread the kibble dough onto the greased cookie sheet until it is approximately one-half inch thick. Place the tray in the oven.

• Bake the dog food for approximately 45 minutes until Trit is brown and firm to the touch. Pull the cookie sheet from the oven and allow to cool.

• Remove the baked "cookie" from the tray and break it into bite-sized pieces for your dog. Store the crunchy dog food in an airtight container in the refrigerator.

Spinach And Salmon Scramble

Ingredients

• 1 teaspoon extra virgin olive oil (EVOO)

• 1/2 can skinless, boneless salmon

• (3 ounces), drained

• 1/2 cup frozen chopped spinach, thawed and drained

• 2 eggs

Instructions:

• In a small nonstick skillet, heat the EVOO over medium heat.

• Add the spinach and salmon and cook until heated through.

• Add the eggs and stir continuously until cooked through, about 2 minutes.

• Let cool slightly and serve in a dog bowl.

Vegan Happy Dog Bowl

Ingredients:

• 1 large sweet potato

• 1 can (15 ounces) black beans, drained and rinsed

• 2/3 cups uncooked brown rice

• 1 1/3 cup water (yields 2 cups cooked)

• 6 kale leaf stems, broken into 1 inch pieces

Instructions:

• Preheat oven to 400F.

• Line baking sheet with tin foil.

• Pierce sweet potato with a fork multiple times around the sweet potato.

• Place on baking sheet and bake for one hour.

• While sweet potato is baking, cook rice: Bring rice and water to a boil in stockpot. Lower temperature and simmer, covered, for about 45 minutes.

• Chop sweet potatoes into small pieces when cooled.

• Combine rice, beans, sweet potatoes, and kale stems and separate into 3 equal servings.

• Serve your pup this delicious and nutritious meal and see how much they love it.

Chicken Rice Balls

Ingredients

• 4-5 C. cooked brown rice

• 16 oz frozen peas

- 2 plain whole chickens, about

- 4 lbs each2 small bunches fresh parsley leaves

- 2 medium orange sweet potatoes (yams), chopped

- 2 small-medium bunches kale, stems removed

- 8 whole carrots, chopped

- 8 eggs

Instructions:

- Roast chicken in 350' oven for about 1 hour 25 minutes or until juices run clear. As chickens are roasting, cook the rice (4 C. water & 2 C. rice) and let cool.

- Peel and chop yams, and carrots, add to a large stock pot with about 1/2 cup water. Add in peas, kale and apple. Allow to boil then simmer until carrots and yams are tender, about 30 minutes. Transfer with a slotted spoon to remove any liquid to a food processor, add fresh parsley and pulse until pureed.

- Cook scrambled eggs, plain.

- Cool chicken, then pick apart and add meat to a large stand mixer. On medium speed, mix until chicken is shredded. Add in cooled rice, veggie puree and eggs . Using an ice cream scooper, scoop out portions onto a lined baking sheet. Flash freeze then place portions in a freezer safe container/baggie.

• To use, keep a day or two worth in your fridge to thaw. I microwave thawed portions for 22 seconds, frozen for about 45 seconds. Feed to your furry baby.

Food Pucks
Ingredients

• 3 cups raw grass-fed beef

• ½ cup coconut oil or grass-fed tallow

• 6 eggs, whole (you use the shell, too)Dog multiple vitamin powder

• ½ teaspoon grey sea salt

• 1 cup bone broth

• ¾ cup ground flax seed, pumpkin seed or hemp meal

• 1 (300 gram) sweet potato6 chicken livers or

• 2 calf livers2 apples, seeds completely removed

Woof Loaf

Ingredients:

• 1 pound lean ground turkey

• 1/2 cup oats

• 1/2 cup chopped carrots

• 2 eggs

• 1/2 cup peas

• 3 hard-boiled eggs

Instructions:

• Preheat your oven to 350°F. In a bowl, mix together the lean ground turkey, chopped carrots, and peas. Both are healthy for cats and dogs, giving them the nutrition they need for strong eyes and good digestion.

• Add the oats and eggs. Mix until the loaf mixture comes together. Oats help your pet's coat shine, and eggs offer extra protein. Lightly grease a loaf pan with olive oil and then add half the mixture to the pan.

• Place the three hard-boiled eggs along the center of the loaf and then cover with the other half of the ground turkey mixture. Pop in the oven and bake for 45 minutes.

• Cut a half-inch slice from the cooled loaf and offer it to your pet. He'll be woofing for seconds! If feeding a slice to your feline, it's a good idea to chop it up before adding it to her feeding dish.

Ingredients

• 2 organic eggsgreen pepper, dicedsmoked salmon, thinly sliced1 oven-safe ramekin

Instructions

• Lightly grease ramekin with a small drizzle of olive oil. Crack eggs directly into ramekin.

• Stir thoroughly with a fork until combined.

• Bake at 350 F for 10 to 12 minutes or until browned on top and cooked completely.

• Allow to cool and serve.

Chicken Casserole

Ingredients

• 2 chicken breasts

• 2 cups chicken broth

• 1 cup chopped vegetables (carrots, green beans, potatoes, broccoli)Oil for frying

• ¼ cup rolled oats

Instructions

• Start by chopping the chicken breasts into bite size pieces and sauté them in oil until cooked.

• Add the chicken broth, rolled oats, and chopped vegetables in the pan and simmer from 10 to 15 minutes.

Chicken Rice Balls

Ingredients

• 4-5 C. cooked brown rice

• 16 oz frozen peas

• 2 plain whole chickens, about

• 4 lbs each2 small bunches fresh parsley leaves

• 2 medium orange sweet potatoes (yams), chopped

• 2 small-medium bunches kale, stems removed

• 8 whole carrots, chopped

• 8 eggs

Instructions

• Roast chicken in 350' oven for about 1 hour 25 minutes or until juices run clear. As chickens are roasting, cook the rice (4 C. water & 2 C. rice) and let cool.

• Peel and chop yams, and carrots, add to a large stock pot with about 1/2 cup water. Add in peas, kale and apple. Allow to boil then simmer until carrots and yams are tender, about 30 minutes. Transfer with a slotted spoon to remove any liquid to a food processor, add fresh parsley and pulse until pureed.

• Cook scrambled eggs, plain.

• Cool chicken, then pick apart and add meat to a large stand mixer. On medium speed, mix until chicken is shredded. Add in cooled rice, veggie puree and eggs . Using an ice cream scooper, scoop out portions onto a lined baking sheet. Flash freeze then place portions in a freezer safe container/baggie.

• To use, keep a day or two worth in your fridge to thaw. I microwave thawed portions for 22 seconds, frozen for about 45 seconds. Feed to your furry baby.

Woof Loaf

Ingredients

• 1 pound lean ground turkey

• 1/2 cup oats

• 1/2 cup chopped carrots

• 2 eggs

• 1/2 cup peas

• 3 hard-boiled eggs

Instructions

• Preheat your oven to 350°F. In a bowl, mix together the lean ground turkey, chopped carrots, and peas. Both are healthy for cats and dogs, giving them the nutrition they need for strong eyes and good digestion.

• Add the oats and eggs. Mix until the loaf mixture comes together. Oats help your pet's coat shine, and eggs offer extra protein. Lightly grease a loaf pan with olive oil and then add half the mixture to the pan.

• Place the three hard-boiled eggs along the center of the loaf and then cover with the other half of the ground turkey mixture. Pop in the oven and bake for 45 minutes.

• Cut a half-inch slice from the cooled loaf and offer it to your pet. He'll be woofing for seconds! If feeding a slice to your feline, it's a good idea to chop it up before adding it to her feeding dish.

Mini Omelettes

Ingredients

• 2 organic eggsgreen pepper,

• dicedsmoked salmon,

• thinly sliced1 oven-safe ramekin

Instructions

• Lightly grease ramekin with a small drizzle of olive oil. Crack eggs directly into ramekin.

• Stir thoroughly with a fork until combined.

• Bake at 350 F for 10 to 12 minutes or until browned on top and cooked completely.

• Allow to cool and serve.

Homemade Chicken Dinner for Dogs

Ingredients:

• 5 pounds chicken

• 2 cups of red cabbage

• 2 apples (skinned)

• 2 cups of spinach

• 5 whole eggs, raw or cooked

• 2 tablespoons olive oil

Instructions:

• You can cook the food, or feed your dog a raw diet. However, with a raw diet you want to make sure you are buying fresh meats which doesn't always happen at a grocery store.

• If you decide to cook it, chop up the chicken and boil in a suitable sized pot for all ingredients until it is almost fully cooked. Reduce to a simmer and add the cabbage, spinach, and apples, diced up. Simmer until the chicken finishes cooking. Remove pot from stove, let cool, then add the eggs and olive oil and stir.

• How long this batch lasts depends on the size of your dog and how many times you feed them each day. Two and a half cups is usually good for a large dog around 60-75 pounds, if you're feeding them twice a day. Keep leftovers in the refrigerator in an airtight container for up to five days.

Homemade Fish Dinner for Dogs

Ingredients:

• 2 pounds of fish fillets

• 1 or 2 cans of pink salmon

• 3 whole eggs, raw or cooked

• 3 cups of diced vegetables Some great choices include cabbage, cooked squash or pumpkin, peas, green beans and kale. You can use two or more.

• 1 cup of cooked rice (white or brown) If your dog tolerates it well. Otherwise try cooked oatmeal, quinoa or lentils.

Instructions:

• Again, you can grind or dice the fish then cook it. Mix the chosen vegetables into a pot of water, bring to a boil and then simmer for about 5 minutes before adding the other ingredients. Mix and let cool. Keep in refrigerator in well sealed container for up to three days, or freeze.

Chicken, Broccoli and Rice Dinner for Dogs

Ingredients:

• 5 pounds of diced chicken

• 5 whole eggs, raw or cooked

• 5 cups cooked rice (white or brown), or again substitute cooked lentils or quinoa

• 3 cups of broccoli, chopped

• 3 tablespoons of olive oil

Instructions:

• Boil chicken and rice until the chicken is almost fully cooked, then add broccoli and simmer until the chicken is finished. Let the meal cool and then add the eggs and oil. This doggy dinner can also be kept in the refrigerator for up to five days.

Homemade Beef Dinner for Dogs
Ingredients:

• 10 pounds of ground beef (or ground turkey)

• 10 whole eggs, raw or cooked

• 5 cups cooked rice (white or brown), cooked lentils, or quinoa

• 3 cups of mixed vegetables

Instructions:

• There are a couple ways that you can do this recipe to make it more fun and interesting for you and your dog. You can either cook the meat and rice/lentils/quinoa up in a pot with water and add the vegetables near the end of cooking.

• The other option is to cook the rice/lentils/quinoa and vegetables until soft, mix everything together with the raw beef and form them into meatballs. Cook meatballs at 400 degrees for about 45 minutes, or until fully cooked.

• You can use these for meals or as an easy to catch snack, once they are cooled. Refrigerate in a sealed container for up to five days.

• One of my three dogs has a very sensitive stomach, so I've taken over making meals for him. My typical recipe follows most closely to this recipe. I combine three pounds of 90 percent lean ground beef, frozen peas, and chicken broth in an Instant Pot and put it on the Meat/Stew setting for one hour. Separately, I prepare two dry cups of Jasmine rice.

• When those are cooked and cooled, I mix everything together in a large mixing bowl and add one can of no salt added green beans and a 29 ounce can of pumpkin. It might take two batches to mix everything thoroughly (at least in the bowl I have). This feeds my 70 pound husky mix for four to five days, depending on how heavy-handed I am at feeding time.

Homemade Doggy Dessert Dinner
Ingredients:

• 2 pounds of chopped up chicken, cooked

• 3 cups of mixed fruit

• 3 cups cooked rice (white or brown), cooked lentils, or quinoa

Instructions:

• Simply mix the ingredients together and serve. Refrigerate for up to five days. This will only yield a small batch, since you don't want to overdo it on the fruit intake.

THE ULTIMATE GUIDE TO HOME SECURITY

How to
Select the Perfect
Door locks

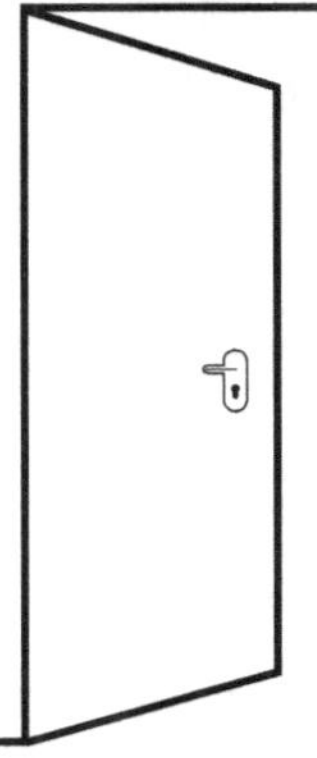